EDGE BOOKS™

GERMAN SHEPHERDS

By Tammy Gagne

Consultant: Jennifer Zablotny, DVM
Member, American Veterinary Medical Association

Capstone
press®

Mankato, Minnesota

Edge Books are published by Capstone Press,
151 Good Counsel Drive, P.O. Box 669, Mankato, Minnesota 56002.
www.capstonepress.com

Library of Congress Cataloging-in-Publication Data
Gagne, Tammy.
    German shepherds / by Tammy Gagne.
    p. cm. — (Edge books. All about dogs.)
    Includes bibliographical references and index.
    ISBN-13: 978-1-4296-1951-6 (hardcover)
    ISBN-10: 1-4296-1951-1 (hardcover)
    1. German shepherd dog — Juvenile literature. I. Title. II. Series.
SF429.G37G34 2009
636.737'6 — dc22   2008001225

Summary: Describes the history, physical features, temperament, and care of
    the German shepherd dog breed.

Editorial Credits
Erika L. Shores, editor; Veronica Bianchini, designer; Marcie Spence,
    photo researcher

Photo Credits
Alamy/David Davies, 21; Nordicphotos, 22; tbkmedia.de, 12
Capstone Press/Karon Dubke, cover, 1, 14, 17 (top), 18, 23, 24, 27, 29
Corbis/Bettmann, 7, 15
Getty Images Inc./General Photographic Agency, 11; Hulton Archive, 5, 6
Photo by Fiona Green, 19, 26
Sally Wallis/123RF, 17 (bottom)
Shutterstock/Lisa F. Young, 9 (bottom); Waldemar Dabrowski, 9 (top)

**Capstone Press thanks Martha Diedrich, dog trainer, for her assistance
    with this book.**

1 2 3 4 5 6 13 12 11 10 09 08

Table of Contents

CHAPTER 1

A FAMOUS DOG

The most famous German shepherd of all time was Rin Tin Tin. This legendary dog starred in more than 25 films in the 1920s. He brought crowds of people to movie theaters across the United States. Rin Tin Tin earned $1,000 a week, had his own limousine, personal chef, and a diamond collar.

Rin Tin Tin was born in France in 1918. His mother and her five-day-old pups survived a World War I (1914-1918) bomb that hit their kennel. U.S. Air Force Corporal Lee Duncan adopted two of these puppies — Rin Tin Tin and his sister Nannette. Duncan brought them home with him to California when the war ended. Nannette died shortly after arriving in the United States.

Rin Tin Tin made the German shepherd dog breed famous.

Lee Duncan named Rin Tin Tin after a French puppet.

In 1922, Rin Tin Tin's talents were discovered when he and Duncan attended a dog show. The German shepherd amazed the crowd by jumping more than 11 feet (3 meters) into the air. Duncan soon began trying to get Rin Tin Tin roles in movies. At this time, a small studio called Warner Brothers was struggling to make money. The studio took a chance on Rin Tin Tin, and the rest is history.

EDGE FACT

According to the American Kennel Club, the shepherd's official name is the German Shepherd Dog.

Another important German shepherd was named Buddy. Buddy became the first guide dog for the blind in the United States in 1928. Buddy's owner, Morris Frank, who was blind, helped open the first school to train guide dogs in the United States a year later.

Today, German shepherds continue to help people with disabilities. These dogs do everything from helping their owners turn on light switches to crossing busy streets.

Morris Frank relied on his guide dog, Buddy, to help with everyday tasks like safely crossing the street.

German shepherds are also the most popular breed used in police work. Shepherds have a keen sense of smell for sniffing out illegal drugs and searching for missing people.

The Right Breed for You?

German shepherds make wonderful pets for the right people. Owning one, however, is a huge responsibility. Shepherds can live 15 years or longer, making ownership a serious commitment. Shepherds can also get into a lot of trouble if they are not trained properly. This large breed can destroy property. Potential owners should decide if they have enough time to care for a shepherd.

EDGE FACT

German shepherds make excellent police dogs because of their intelligence and eagerness to please their master.

The best way to find a German shepherd puppy is through a breeder. Local German shepherd breed clubs can recommend a good breeder. These breeders sell dogs that feature the best qualities of the breed.

Adoption is also an option for finding a shepherd. Adult dogs are often already trained. They are usually calmer than puppies. Local animal shelters or rescue groups can help you find a dog in need of a home.

Patient shepherds are always ready for action while on police duty.

CHAPTER 2

GERMAN SHEPHERD HISTORY

A former German military officer named Max Emil Frederick von Stephanitz introduced the German shepherd to the public. The German shepherds he bred worked as herding dogs on his farm in the late 1800s. Herding dogs help control and protect large groups of farm animals such as sheep.

Von Stephanitz later became the first president of the German shepherd breed club. He also played a role in writing the first German shepherd breed standard. A breed standard describes the ideal characteristics for a dog breed.

Joining the Fight

When Word War I began, von Stephanitz offered some of his dogs to the German army. At first the soldiers laughed at the idea of dogs helping them fight the war. But the dogs performed well. German shepherds carried messages, located wounded soldiers, and stood watch for their new masters.

German shepherds served at the side of German soldiers in World War I.

German shepherds compete in American Kennel Club events.

Rin Tin Tin was a direct descendant of von Stephanitz's shepherds. His fame sparked the German shepherd's rise in popularity. Everyone on both sides of the Atlantic Ocean wanted a German shepherd for a pet.

POPULARITY SOARS

The first German shepherd to compete in an American dog show was named Queen of Switzerland. This dog was registered with the American Kennel Club (AKC) in 1908. The German Shepherd Dog Club of America formed in 1922.

Demand for German shepherds was soaring, but von Stephanitz realized that this could be a problem for the breed. He worried people would breed and sell poor quality shepherds. Germany started sending fewer dogs to the United States. But it was too late. Americans were breeding their own German shepherds as quickly as they could.

The puppies produced lacked many important qualities of the breed. The German shepherd's trustworthy nature was disappearing. Its health was also declining. The most important factors in breeding – health and **temperament** – were being pushed to the bottom of breeders' priority lists.

temperament — the way an animal usually acts or responds to situations

In 1929, the United States entered a time of great poverty called the Great Depression. During this period many owners could not afford to care for the shepherds they bought. Many dogs were left on the streets to fend for themselves. When Rin Tin Tin died in 1932, interest in the breed had fallen considerably.

In the 1950s, another soon-to-be famous German shepherd appeared on the scene. A relative of Rin Tin Tin began playing his character in a TV series called *The Adventures of Rin Tin Tin*. This dog helped recharge the public's love for the breed. German shepherds became more popular than ever.

Over the years, the German shepherd has remained one of the most popular dogs in the United States. The German Shepherd Dog Club of America teaches people where to find dogs that most closely match the breed standard. Today, the United States has many responsible breeders who produce healthy and strong German shepherds.

Two German shepherds related to the first Rin Tin Tin played the role of the famous dog in the TV series.

EDGE FACT

Today, Daphne Hereford breeds German shepherds in Texas that are descendants of the original Rin Tin Tin.

CHAPTER 3

COURAGEOUS AND SMART

A German shepherd is the picture of strength and courage. Shepherds have solid, muscular bodies. These dogs stand between 22 and 26 inches (56 and 66 centimeters) tall. They weigh between 55 and 95 pounds (25 and 43 kilograms). Female shepherds are smaller than males.

A shepherd's face has distinct features. Its eyes are dark and almond-shaped. Its ears are pointed and stand upright. A dog with drooping ears cannot compete in dog shows. Likewise, a show dog's nose must be black.

A German shepherd has a double coat. A softer layer of hair lies underneath a coarser one. The outer coat is dense with straight hair. The hair on the dog's neck is longer and thicker than hair on its head, body, and legs. All shepherds have long, bushy tails.

Most German shepherds are black and tan. Shepherds can be other colors such as black and cream, black and silver, solid black, or sable. A sable dog's hair is tipped with black. Some German shepherds are white, but they aren't allowed to compete in dog shows.

Tall, pointed ears are a noticeable feature of the German shepherd breed.

EDGE FACT

German shepherds are known as a "one person" breed. They tend to show the most affection to their main caretaker.

German shepherds are loyal and kind to their families.

Temperament

The German shepherd's temperament is a big part of its appeal. The shepherd is friendly but is always watchful of strangers. If someone threatens its family, this dog is the first to stand between the stranger and those it loves. For this reason, shepherds make excellent guard dogs.

German shepherds are very intelligent. They enjoy pleasing their owners and have a natural desire to protect them. Because shepherds are so smart, they do best when they have a purpose. Left alone all day with little to do, shepherds might chew furniture or bark nonstop. These dogs need plenty of exercise before they are left alone for long periods of time.

CHAPTER 4

CARING FOR A GERMAN SHEPHERD

Owning a dog is a big responsibility. The needs of a German shepherd exceed those of many other breeds. This responsibility must be considered before deciding that this breed is right for you.

Training a German Shepherd

All dogs need training, but it is even more important for German shepherds than many other breeds. Shepherds have a strong desire to protect their owners, and they need training to do so properly. Alerting an owner that the mail carrier is coming is fine. But tackling the mail carrier on the front porch is not.

Owners should start by teaching their puppies commands such as "sit," "stay," and "come." Puppies need to learn that their owners are in charge. By following these commands consistently, a dog displays respect for its owner's **authority**.

authority — the right to do something or to tell others what to do

Owners spend many hours training their German shepherds.

21

Socializing a German shepherd is just as necessary as training it. A German shepherd puppy should be introduced to as many different people and dogs as possible. A socialized puppy learns to be relaxed around people other than its owner. Puppies also learn how to get along with other dogs.

German shepherds need to learn how to behave around children.

socialize — to train to get along with people and other dogs

What a Shepherd Needs

You will need to buy important items for your dog. These items include a leash and collar, a set of dishes, and a place to sleep.

You can find everything your German shepherd needs at a pet supply store. Leashes and collars come in a variety of materials. Leather is best for this breed. Leather is strong and won't wear out quickly.

Stainless steel bowls are a favorite choice for many German shepherd owners. These dishes can be washed easily and won't break if they are dropped. They will also hold up to being chewed on by your dog.

Some owners combine both wet and dry food for their dog's meals.

24

A German shepherd may enjoy having a dog bed, but a dog crate may be a better choice. Metal or plastic crates keep dogs safe when their owners aren't at home. Many dogs feel secure having a place of their own.

Some owners feel that crates are too much like cages and prefer not to use them. These owners might decide to allow their dogs to sleep on their beds. Some dog trainers, however, think a dog shouldn't be allowed on the bed. The trainers feel it makes it harder for the dog to understand that it's not the boss.

Feeding a German Shepherd

German shepherds must eat healthy food each day. But eating too much food can cause a dog to become overweight. Follow the instructions on the dog's food bag to determine the right amount for your pet.

Many owners feed their shepherds either dry or wet dog food. Some owners feed their German shepherds raw foods such as meat and vegetables.

A dog's dishes should be emptied and cleaned daily. Never add food or water to what your dog left in its bowl. Dishes that aren't washed daily can grow dangerous **bacteria** and make your dog sick.

bacteria — microscopic living things; some bacteria cause disease.

Because a shepherd's thick coat sheds constantly, regular brushing is necessary.

Grooming a German Shepherd

German shepherds shed heavily. They need daily brushing. If shepherds aren't brushed, they'll leave hair on furniture, clothing, and anything else they come near.

A dog's ears and teeth must also be kept clean. Owners can find ear cleaner and toothpaste made for dogs at most pet supply stores. Don't use human toothpaste on your German shepherd. Because dogs swallow their toothpaste, human products make them sick.

Finally, owners must clip their German shepherd's toenails regularly. Long nails can catch in carpeting and clothing.

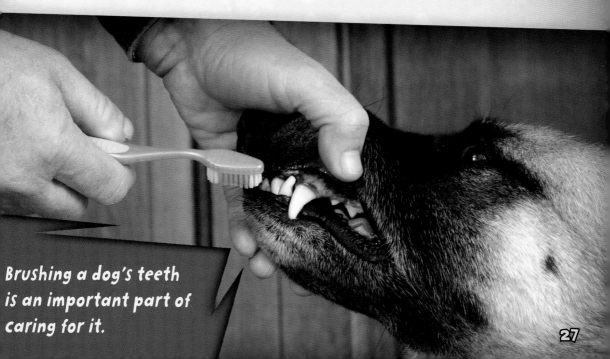

Brushing a dog's teeth is an important part of caring for it.

Keeping a German Shepherd Healthy

The best way to keep your German shepherd healthy is to take it to a veterinarian. Dogs need to visit a vet yearly for vaccinations and a checkup.

Vets can check German shepherds for diseases common in the breed. Shepherds are more likely than some breeds to have hip dysplasia. The hip bones of a dog with this condition do not fit together properly. Hip dysplasia causes pain and makes movement difficult.

Vets can also spay or neuter your German shepherd. These simple operations prevent dogs from ever having puppies. Fewer unwanted puppies helps control the pet population. It also lowers the animal's risk for some diseases, including cancer.

German shepherds can make wonderful pets. They offer their love, loyalty, and protection to their owners and ask nothing in return. Owners show their love for their German shepherds by keeping them looking and feeling their best.

Vets feel the hips of shepherds to check for signs of hip dysplasia.

Glossary

authority (uh-THOR-uh-tee) — the right to do something or to tell others what to do

bacteria (bak-TEER-ee-uh) — microscopic living things; some bacteria cause disease.

breed (BREED) — a certain kind of animal within an animal group; breed also means to mate and raise a certain kind of animal.

breeder (BREE-duhr) — someone who breeds and raises dogs or other animals

descendant (di-SEN-duhnt) — a dog's offspring and family members born to those offspring

socialize (SOH-shuh-lize) — to train to get along with people and other dogs

temperament (TEMP-ur-muhnt) — the combination of a dog's behavior and personality; the way an animal usually acts or responds to situations shows its temperament.

vaccination (vak-suh-NAY-shun) — a shot of medicine that protects animals from a disease

Read More

Allen, Jean. *German Shepherds.* Dog Breeds. North Mankato, Minn.: Smart Apple Media, 2003.

Fiedler, Julie. *German Shepherd Dogs.* Tough Dogs. New York: PowerKids Press, 2006.

Gray, Susan H. *German Shepherds.* Domestic Dogs. Mankato, Minn.: Child's World, 2008.

Internet Sites

FactHound offers a safe, fun way to find Internet sites related to this book. All of the sites on FactHound have been researched by our staff.

Here's how:

1. Visit *www.facthound.com*
2. Choose your grade level.
3. Type in this book ID **1429619511** for age-appropriate sites. You may also browse subjects by clicking on letters, or by clicking on pictures and words.
4. Click on the **Fetch It** button.

FactHound will fetch the best sites for you!

Index